Naaman's Spots

Fairfield P.N.E.U. School
(Backwell) Ltd.,
Farleigh Road,
Backwell, Bristol.

© Copyright 1994 by Kevin Mayhew Ltd.

KEVIN MAYHEW LTD
Rattlesden Bury St Edmunds
Suffolk England
IP30 0SZ

ISBN 0 86209 566 2
Catalogue No. 1108127

Printed in Great Britain

Naaman's Spots

Retold from Scripture by Pat Rissen and illustrated by Arthur Baker

Kevin Mayhew

Naaman was the commander of the
Syrian Army. The King of Syria was
very pleased with Naaman
because he was a great soldier,
and he could always beat the army
of God's chosen people,
the Israelites.

During one of their battles, the Syrians captured a little Israelite girl. Naaman took the little girl home to his wife, where she had to work hard cooking the meals and keeping Naaman's house clean and tidy.

Naaman was a clever soldier, but he had one terrible problem. He was covered from head to toe with big spots. The spots worried him so much that he visited all the best doctors in Syria, trying to find a cure.

But they all looked at his spots and shook their heads sadly. None of them could help him.

The horrible spots made Naaman very unhappy. The little servant girl noticed how sad he was.

One day, seeing Naaman looking miserable, she said to her mistress, 'I wish the master would go to see God's prophet Elisha, who lives in my country. I'm sure that he could cure the master's spots. For our God loves everyone – even the enemies of his people.'

When Naaman heard this, he went to his King and told him what the little Israelite girl had said. And the King gave Naaman a letter to take to the King of Israel.

The letter said: 'This is to introduce my officer Naaman. I want you to cure him of his spots.'

Naaman and his servants set off for Israel, taking with them chests full of gold, silver and fine clothing as gifts for the prophet Elisha.

When Naaman reached Israel, he took his letter to the King. When the King read it he was very upset. He stared hard at Naaman's big spots and said, 'How on earth can the King of Syria expect ME to cure this man? Does he think that I am GOD with the power of life and death?'

'I think he's trying to start a quarrel with me.' And he sent Naaman away.

When God's prophet Elisha heard what had happened, he told the King to send Naaman to see him. So Naaman hopped into his chariot, and hurried to Elisha's house.

But when he knocked on the door, Elisha did not come out.

Instead, he sent his servant out to speak to Naaman. The servant told Naaman to go and wash himself in the River Jordan, not once, not twice, but SEVEN times, if he wanted to be free of his spots.

Naaman was very, very angry and he left Elisha's house in a rage.

'I thought Elisha would at least have come out and looked at my spots and prayed to that God of his,' he muttered crossly. 'The rivers at home are just as good as any old river in Israel. I'm sure I could have washed in them and been cured.'

So Naaman sat on a rock and sulked. His servants all waited patiently until his temper began to cool down. Then they got together and said, 'Sir, why don't you just *try* washing yourself in the River Jordan? It might work! After all, if Elisha had told you to do something *difficult* you would have done it.'

'Oh all right,' agreed Naaman, though he still wasn't very enthusiastic about the idea.

He set off for the River Jordan, and on the river bank he undressed quickly. While his servants stood by to keep count, Naaman jumped into the water.

Naaman washed himself just as Elisha had instructed.

SPLISH,
  SPLASH,
    SPLOOSH!

One
  two
    three
      four
        five
          six

SEVEN TIMES!

And when he jumped out of the water for the last time, Naaman knew that his little servant girl had been speaking the truth. The God of Israel really did love everyone, even the enemies of his people.

For when Naaman jumped out of the water for the last time, every one of the horrible spots had disappeared.

Naaman had been cured!

Note for parents:
You can find this story
in the Old Testament 2 Kings,
chapter 5.